FRANKLIN'S WAY TO WEALTH;

OR,

"𝔓𝔬𝔬𝔯 𝔕𝔦𝔠𝔥𝔞𝔯𝔡 𝔍𝔪𝔭𝔯𝔬𝔳𝔢𝔡, &𝔠."

A NEW EDITION:

CORRECTED AND ENLARGED BY BOB SHORT; AND
ADORNED WITH COPPER-PLATES.

𝔏𝔬𝔫𝔡𝔬𝔫:

PRINTED BY W. DARTON, Jun.
58, HOLBORN HILL,
1814.

INTRODUCTION.

Dr. Franklin, wishing to collect into one piece, all the pithy sayings upon various subjects, which he had inserted in the course of publishing the Almanacks called " Poor Richard," introduces Father Abraham for this purpose. Hence it is, that Poor Richard is so often quoted.

Poor Richard (Saunders) and Father Abraham have proved, in America, that they are no common preachers. And shall we, brother Englishmen, refuse good sense and useful knowledge, because they come from the other side of the water? no surely.————

THE

WAY TO WEALTH.

I HAVE heard that nothing gives an author such great pleasure, as to find his works respectfully quoted by others. Judge, then, how much I must have been gratified by an incident I am going to relate to you. I stopped my horse, lately, where a great number of people were collected at an auction of merchants' goods. The hour of the sale not being come, they were conversing on the badness of the times; and one of the company called to a plain, clean, old man, with white locks, and said, ' Pray Father Abraham, what think you of the times ? Will not those heavy taxes quite ruin the country! How shall we be ever able to pay them ? What would you advise us to do ?'——Father Abraham stood up, and replied, ' If you would have my advice, I will give it you in short; " for a word to the wise is enough," as Poor Richard says. They joined in desiring him to speak his mind, and gathering round him, he proceeded as follows:

' Friends,' says he, ' the taxes are indeed very heavy; and, if those laid on by the government were the *only* ones we had to pay,

London, Published by Will.ᵐ Darton, Holborn Hill Oct.ʳ 30.1823.

we might more easily discharge them; but we have many others, and much more grievous to some of us. We are taxed *twice* as much by our idleness, *three* times as much by our pride, and *four* times as much by our folly; and from these taxes the commissioners cannot ease or deliver us by allowing an abatement. However, let us hearken to good advice, and something may be done for us; "God helps them that help themselves," as Poor Richard says.

I. 'It would be thought a hard government that should tax its people one-tenth part of their time to be employed in its service; but idleness taxes many of us much more; sloth, by bringing on diseases, absolutely shortens life.

"Sloth, like rust, consumes faster than labour wears, while the used key is always bright," as Poor Richard says.—"But, dost thou love life? then do not squander time, for that is the stuff life is made of," as Poor Richard says.—How much more than is necessary do we spend in sleep! forgetting that "the sleeping fox catches no poultry, and that there will be sleeping enough in the grave," as Poor Richard says.

"If time be of all things the most precious, wasting time must be" as poor Richard says, "the greatest prodigality;" since, as he elsewhere tells us, "Lost time is never found again; and what we call time enough, always proves little enough." Let us then up and be doing, and doing to the purpose: so by dili-

gence shall we do more with less perplexity.
" Sloth makes all things difficult, but industry all easy: and he that riseth late, must trot
all day, and shall scarce overtake his business
at night; while laziness travels so slowly, that
poverty soon overtakes him. Drive thy business, let not that drive thee; and early to
bed, and early to rise, makes a man healthy,
wealthy, and wise," as Poor Richard says.

' So what signifies wishing and hoping for
better times? We may make these times better, if we bestir ourselves. " Industry need
not wish, and he that lives upon hope will
die fasting. There are no gains without pains;
then help hands, for I have no lands;" or if
I have, they are smartly taxed. " He that
hath a trade, hath an estate; and he that hath
a calling, hath an office of profit and honour,"
as Poor Richard says; but then the trade
must be worked at, and the calling well fol-
lowed, or neither the estate nor the office will
enable us to pay our taxes,—

If we are industrious, we shall never starve;
for at the working man's house hunger looks
in, but dares not enter." Nor will the bailiff
or the constable enter, for " industry pays
debts, while despair increaseth them." What,
though you have found no treasure, nor has
any rich relation left you a legacy. " Diligence is the mother of good luck, and God
gives all things to industry. Then plow deep,
while sluggards sleep, and you shall have corn
to sell and to keep." Work while it is called

to-day, for you know not how much you may
be hindered to-morrow. "One to-day is
worth two to-morrows," as Poor Richard
says, and farther, "Never leave that till to-
morrow, which you can do to-day."—If you
were a servant, would you not be ashamed
that a good master should catch you idle?
Are you then your own master? be ashamed
to catch yourself idle, when there is so much
to be done for yourself, your family your
country, and your king.

Handle your tools without mittens; remember, that "The cat in gloves catches no mice,"
as Poor Richard says. It is true, there is
much to be done, and, perhaps, you are weak-
handed; but stick to it steadily, and you will
see great effects; for "Constant dropping
wears away stones; and by diligence and patience the mouse ate in two the cable; and little
strokes fell great oaks."

'Methinks I hear some of you say, "Must
a man afford himself no leisure? I will tell
thee, my friend, what Poor Richard says,
"Employ thy time well, if thou meanest to
gain leisure; and since thou art not sure of a
minute, throw not away an hour." Leisure
is time for doing something useful; this leisure the diligent man will obtain, but the lazy
man never; for, "A life of leisure and a life
of laziness are two different things. Many,
without labour, would live by their wits only,
but they break for want of stock;" whereas
industry gives comfort, plenty, and respect.

London, Published by Will'm Darton, Holborn Hill, Oct'r 20, 1823.

" Fly pleasures and they will follow you.
The diligent spinner has a large shift; and now
I have a sheep and a cow, every body bids me
good-morrow."

II. 'But with our industry we must like-
wise be steady, settled, and careful; and oversee our own affairs with our own eyes, and not
trust too much to others: for, as Poor Richard
says,

> " I never saw an oft-removed tree,
> Nor yet an oft-removed family,
> That throve so well as those that settled be."

And again, " *Three* removes are as bad as a
fire," and again, " Keep thy shop, and thy
shop will keep thee:" and again, " If you
would have your business done, go; if not,
send." And again,

"He that by the plow would thrive,
Himself must either hold or drive."

'And again, "The eye of the master will do
more work than both his hands:" and again,
"Want of care does us more damage than
want of knowledge;" and again, "not to
oversee workmen, is to leave them your purse
open."

'Trusting too much to others care is the
ruin of many; for, "In the affairs of this
world, men are saved not by faith, but by the
want of it;" but a man's own care is profitable; for, "If you would have a faithful servant, and one that you like,—serve *yourself*.
A little neglect may breed great mischief; for
want of a nail the shoe was lost; and for want
of a shoe the horse was lost; and for want of
a horse the rider was lost;" being overtaken
and slain by the enemy; all for want of a little care about a horse-shoe nail.

III. 'So much for industry, my friends, and
attention to one's own business; but to these
we must add *frugality*, if we would make
our industry more certainly successful. A
man may, if he knows not how to save as he
gets, "keep his nose all his life to the grind-
stone, and die not worth a groat at last. A
fat kitchen makes a lean will;" and,

"Many estates are spent in the getting,
Since women for tea forsook spinning and knitting,
And men to get punch forsook hewing and splitting."

"If you would be wealthy, think of *saving*,
as well as of *getting*. The Indies have not

made Spain rich, because her out-goes are greater than her in-comes."

'Away, then, with your expensive follies, and you will not then have so much cause to complain of hard times, heavy taxes, and chargeable families; for,

> " Women and wine, game and deceit,
> Make the wealth small, and the want great."

And farther, " What maintains one vice, would bring up two children." You may think perhaps, that a little tea, or a little punch now and then, diet a little more costly, clothes a little finer, and a little entertainment now and then, can be no great matter; but remember, " Many a little makes a mickle." Beware of *little* expences; " A small leak will sink a great ship," as Poor Richard says; and again, who dainties love shall beggars prove;" and moreover, " Fools makes feasts, and wise men eat them." Here you are all got together to this sale of fineries and nick-nacks. You call them goods, but, if you do not take care, they will prove *evils* to some of you. You expect they will be sold cheap, and, perhaps, they may for less than they cost; but, if you have no occasion for them, they must be dear to you. Remember what Poor Richard says, " Buy what thou hast no need of, and ere long thou shalt sell thy necessaries." And again, " At a great penny-worth pause awhile;" he means, that perhaps the cheapness is apparent only, and not real;

or the bargain, by straitening thee in thy business, may do thee more harm than good. For, in another place, he says, "Many have been ruined by buying good pennyworths." Again, "It is foolish to lay out money in a purchase of repentance;" and yet this folly is practised every day at auctions, for want of minding the Almanack. Many a one, for the sake of finery on the back, have gone with a hungry belly, and half starved their families; "Silks and satins, scarlet and velvets, put out the kitchen fire," as Poor Richard says.

These are not the *necessaries* of life; they can scarcely be called the conveniences; and yet only because they look pretty, how many want to have them?—By these, and other extravagancies, the genteel are reduced to poverty, and forced to borrow of those whom they formerly despised, but who, through industry and frugality, have maintained their standing; in which case it appears plainly, that "A ploughman on his legs is higher than a gentleman on his knees," as Poor Richard says. Perhaps they have had a small estate left them, which they knew not the getting of; they think "it is day, and will never be night:" that a little to be spent out of so much is not worth minding; but "Always taking out of the meal-tub, and never putting in, soon comes to the bottom," as Poor Richard says; and then, "When the well is dry, they know the want of water." But this they might have known before, if they had taken his advice.

"If you would know the value of money, go and try to borrow some; for he that goes a borrowing, goes a sorrowing," as, Poor Richard says; and, indeed, so does he that lends to such people, when he goes to get it in again. Poor Dick farther advises, and says,

> "Fond pride of dress is sure a very curse,
> E're fancy you consult, consult your purse."

'And again, "Pride is as loud a beggar as Want, and a great deal more saucy." When you have bought one fine thing, you must buy ten more, that your appearance may be all of a piece; but Poor Dick says, "It is easier to suppress the first desire, than to satisfy all that follow it." And it is as truly folly for the poor to ape the rich, as for the frog to swell, in order to equal the ox.

> "Vessels large may venture more,
> But little boats should keep near shore,"

It is, however, a folly soon punished; for, as Poor Richard says, "Pride that dines on vanity, sups on contempt;—Pride breakfasted with Plenty, dined with Poverty, and supped with Infamy." And, after all, of what use is this pride of appearance, for which so much is risked, and so much is suffered? It cannot promote health, nor ease pain; it makes no increase of merit in the person, but creates envy, and hastens misfortune.

London, Published by Will.ⁿ Darton, Holborn Hill, Oct.ʳ 20, 1823.

' But what madness it must be to run in
debt for these superfluities? We are offered
by the terms of this sale, *six* months credit;
and that, perhaps, has induced some of us to
attend it, because we cannot spare the ready
money, and hope now to be fine without it,
But, ah! think what you do when you run in
debt; you give to another power over your
liberty. If you cannot pay at the time, you
will be ashamed to see your creditor; you
will be in fear when you speak to him; you
will make poor pitiful sneaking excuses, and,
by degrees come to lose your veracity, and
sink into base, downright lying: for, " The
second vice is lying, the first is running in
debt," as Poor Richard says; and again, to
the same purpose, " Lying rides upon Debt's

back:" whereas a free-born Englishman ought not to be ashamed nor afraid to see or speak to any man living. But poverty often deprives a man of all spirit and virtue. " It is hard for an empty bag to stand upright."

What would you think of that prince, or of that government, who should issue an edict forbidding you to dress like a gentleman or gentlewoman, on pain of imprisonment or servitude? Would you not say that you were free, have a right to dress as you please, and that such an edict would be a breach of your privileges, and such a government tyrannical? And yet you are about to put yourself under that tyranny, when you run in debt for such dress! Your creditor has authority at his pleasure, to deprive you of your liberty, by confining you in gaol for life, or by selling you for a servant if you should not be able to pay him.

When you have got your bargain, you may, perhaps, think little of payment; but, as Poor Richard says, " Creditors have better memories than debtors; creditors are a superstitious sect, great observers of set days and times." The day comes round before you are aware, and the demand is made before you are prepared to satisfy it: or, if you bear your debt in mind, the term, which at first seemed so long, will, as it lessens, appear extremely short: Time will seem to have added wings to his heels as well as his shoulders. Those have a short Lent, who owe money to be paid at Easter." At present, perhaps, you may think yourselves in thriving circumstances, and that you can bear a little axtravagance without injury: but,

> " For age and want save while you may,
> No morning sun lasts a whole day."

'Gain may be temporary and uncertain; but ever, while you live, expence is constant and certain; and "It is easier to build two chimneys, than to keep one in fuel," as Poor Richard says: so, "Rather go to bed supperless, than rise in debt,"

> Get what you can, and what you get hold,
> 'Tis the stone that will turn all your lead into gold.

And when you have got the Philosopher's stone, sure you will no longer complain of bad times, or the difficulty of paying taxes.

IV. 'This doctrine, my friends, is reason and wisdom; but, after all, do not depend too much upon your own industry, frugality, and prudence, though excellent things; for they may all be blasted without the blessing of Heaven; and therefore, ask that blessing humbly, and be not uncharitable to those that at present seem to want it, but comfort and help them. Remember Job suffered, and was afterwards prosperous.

'And now to conclude, "Experience keeps a dear school, but fools will learn in no other," as Poor Richard says, and scarce

in that; for it is true, " We may give advice,
but we cannot give conduct." However, remember this, "They that will not be coun-
selled cannot be helped;" and farther, that
" If you will not hear Reason, she will surely
rap your knuckles," as Poor Richard says.'

Thus the old gentleman ended his harangue.
The people heard it, and approved the doctrine, and immediately practised the contrary,
just as if it had been a common sermon; for
the auction opened, and they began to buy
extravagantly.—I found the good man had
thoroughly studied my Almanacks, and di-
gested all I had dropt on those topics during
the course of twenty-five years. The fre-
quent mention he made of me must have
tired any one else; but my vanity was won-

derfully delighted with it, though I was conscious that not a tenth part of the wisdom was my own, which he ascribed to me; but rather the gleanings that I had made of the sense of all ages and nations. However, I resolved to be the better for the echo of it; and, though I at first determined to buy stuff for a new coat, I went away, resolved to wear my old one a little longer. Reader, if thou wilt do the same, thy profit will be as great as mine.——I am, as ever, thine to serve thee,

RICHARD SAUNDERS.

HOW TO MAKE

MUCH OF A LITTLE,

Earnestly addrsssed to the Industrious Poor,

By BOB. SHORT.

THE poor man who *roasts* or *broils* his meat—throws it half into the fire.

The poor man who *boils* it—throws half away in the water.

The poor man who turns it into *broth*, with a little flour, oatmeal, rice, or pease, according to their price, wants the less bread, and has twice the quantity for his money.

Herbs, such as *carrots, celery, turnips,* and some

cabbage and *onions*, but especially *leeks*, if first fried till a little brown in the fat from the broth, and then boiled therein, will make a rich feast at a small expence.

Onions are the best herbs. The idolatrous Egyptians worshipped them;—better worship *them* than the *gin-bottle*.

The poor always get the best penny-worths who buy in the open market; and bargains are always cheapest at the latter end of the day. When honest men have done their work, better go to *market* than the *ale-house*.

The poor who deal on trust may expect to be sometimes *cheated;* for too many shop-keepers think they mean to *cheat* them; therefore they endeavour to be before-hand with them. The *ready* penny always fetches the best bargain.

They that can scarce keep themselves or a child, should never keep a *dog*.

Gin is *poison:*—he that drinks it gives himself false spirits for a time, but rots his liver all the while. If a *gin-maker* be not the greatest enemy to the public, a *gin-drinker* is the greatest enemy to himself and family.

One penny-worth of *broth*, *milk*, or even *water-gruel*, or *beer*, to a hard-working man in the morning, is worth twelve penny-worth of *tea*. If tea be good for them who eat too much, it is ruin to them who eat but *little*. Let the poor be at half the expence for *beer* as they are for *tea*, and they will be able to do twice the work.

Sugar and tea were never in general use till the *eighteenth* century; since the poor have been *tea-*drinkers, half of them have been beggared and starved.

The *general* complaint is, *Times are hard!* Why

then make them *harder still?* A *good* man in bad times, will live ten times better, than a *bad* man in good times.

We often say, *Taxes are heavy!* That may be true; but by whom are we taxed most? Let a man reckon whether many are not taxed *twice* as much by their folly, *three* time as much by their drunkenness, and *four* times as much by their laziness, than they are by the government; and then say if they have a right to complain, because the shoe pinches, when they made it upon their *own* last.

Let the poor do good to themselves at home, and then they will find good in being at home.—It is a true proverb—" God helps them that help themselves."

> Desire not *riches,* they bewitch,
> *Contentment* makes a poor man *rich.*

Industry will make a man a purse, and Frugality give him strings to it. This purse will cost him nothing. They that have it, will only draw the strings as Frugality directs, and will always find an useful penny at the bottom of it.

The servants of Industry are known by their livery; it is always clean and wholesome; look at the ragged and dirty slaves of Laziness, and then ask who serves the *best* master?

The fear of God will make a man think well and act well; and when he needs it, God will provide him a friend.

The man who laughs with you at *the fear of God,* is your worst enemy, and teaches you to be your *own* enemy also. Beware of such.

Remember Sin is the greatest evil; salvation by Jesus Christ the greatest good; and Grace to change the heart, the poor man's richest treasure. Let the poor man then find his way to the cheapest market on a *Saturday;* to that place of worship where he can meet with the best advice on a *Sunday;* and go like an honest man to his labour on the *Monday;* and following these simple rules, he will be happy twice over; happy in *time,* and happy to all *Eternity.*——B. Short.

ALPHABETICAL MAXIMS

Worthy the remembrance and regard of all;

SELECTED BY BOB SHORT.

A.

A Firm Faith is the best Divinity—a good Life the best Philosophy—a clear Conscience the best Law—Honesty the best Policy—and Temperance the best Physic.

Always make your Jest so that it end not in Earnest.

All Fools are not Knaves, but all Knaves are Fools.

Anger may look into the Breast of a *wise* Man, but only rest in the Bosom of *Fools.*

Accuse not Fortune when thou art in the Fault thyself.

A clear Conscience fears no Accusation.

A great many employ the first of their Years to make their last miserable.

All Men of Estates are only Trustees to the poor and distressed, and will be so rewarded when they are to give an account.

London, Published by Will.ᵐ Darton, Holborn Hill.
Oct.ʳ 20 1823.

A good man passeth by an Offence, and a noble Spirit scorneth Revenge.

A Man without Secrecy is an open Letter for every one to read.

B.

Beauty without Virtue is like Poison concealed in a Gold Box.

Beware of a fine Tongue, if it is accustomed to flattery.

By taking Revenge, a Man is but even with his Enemy; but in passing it over he is superior.

Believe not all are evil that are evil spoken of.

Be as careful of what you *say* as of what you *do*.

Better prevent a Quarrel before hand, than revenge it afterwards.

Better break your Word, than do Evil, by keeping it.

Boasting may gain Applause from Fools, but it makes a wise Man blush.

Better be alone, than in bad Company.

Better go to bed Supperless than rise in Debt.

Benevolence is commendable in all persons.

Bear great Things that you may not repine at small.

Bear what is inevitable without murmuring.

Begin to be good in Time, it cannot be too soon.

C.

Cease to be Vicious and you'll cease to be afraid.

Custom is the Plague of wise Men, and the Idol of Fools.

Compasion and benevolence are godlike virtues.

Chuse not a Friend over thy Cups.

Courage and Clemency should never be separated.

Courage is the Champion of Justice, and never ought to be exerted but in a righteous cause.

Conscience is a terror to evil doers, but a comforter to good men.

Causeless Suspicion often occasions the suspected to do Evil, though they always did well before.

Count the World not only an Inn, but an Hospital, and a Place not only to live but also to die in.

Content and health are the poor man's wealth.

Charity is Friendship in Common, and Friendship is Charity inclosed.

D.

Do nothing to day that may bring Repentance to-morrow.

Denying a Fault doubles it.

Die to sin daily, that you may not die for it eternally.

Death and Life are in the Power of the Tongue.

Delay is disagreeable, but may prove the Parent of Wisdom.

Deliberate long on what thou canst do but once.

Defer not Charities till Death; he that doth so is rather liberal of another man's wealth than his own.

Days of pleasure too often bring on Evenings of Repentance.

Diligence is the Mother of Good-luck.

Do well, and fear neither Man nor Devil.

Doing Justice to worthy Qualities is a Credit to our Judgement.

Diamonds have Flaws, and Roses have their thorns.

Drive thy Business, let not thy Business drive thee.

E.

External Beauty will often captivate, but internal Merit secures the Conquest.

Early to Bed and early to rise, makes a Man healthy, wealthy, and wise.

Evil habits are better conquered to-day than to-morrow.

Evil Company make the good bad, and the bad worse.

Experience and instruction are the parents of true wisdom.

Extention spoils the Bow, Relaxation the Mind.

Evil Dispositions need no Tutors.

Every Medal hath its reverse; few Conveniences without inconvenience.

Emulation is a great Incitement to industry.

Envy too often begets hatred and revenge.

Experience is the best adviser; but it is better to learn by others than our own.

F.

Friendship is best tried by adversity.

A Friend in need is a Friend indeed.

Forget others Faults, and remember thine own.

Fine Sense and elevated Sense are not so useful as *Common Sense*.

Frugality is a Fortune, and Industry a good Estate.

Fortune is like a Bubble, which often breaks while it is shining.—Fortune flatters only to deceive.

Fortitude is the medium betwixt fear and boldness.

Fortitude without Wisdom, is but Rashness;—Wisdom without Justice, is but Craftiness.

Real Friends are like ghosts and apparitions, what many persons talk of but few ever saw.

G.

Gratitude is a Duty none can be excused from, because it is always in our own disposal.

Good-Thoughts should always be encouraged to prevent bad actions.

Good-nature is more agreeable in Conversation than Wit, and gives a certain Air to the Countenance, which is more amiable than Beauty.

Greedy Dispositions often lose what they possess.

Gaming, like a Quicksand, swallows up a Man in a Moment; while it blinds the green-horn, at the same time it makes the Sharper quick-sighted.

Good-nature is of all Virtues and qualities of the Mind the greatest, being the Character of the Deity.

Gentleness is the best way to make a man loved and respected by all.

Gratitude preserves old Friendship and procures new.

Gentle replies to scurrilous Language is the most severe Revenge.

To be, do, and get good keep daily in view,
And you'll always find something praiseworthy to do.

H.

Have nothing to do with Men in a Passion, for Men are not like Iron, to be wrought upon when hot.

He that goes a borrowing goes a sorrowing.

He that confesseth his Sins, and mendeth not, is a praying hypocrite.

He that is proud, breakfasteth on Vanity, dineth on Folly, and suppeth on Contempt.

He that mocketh the Lame, is either a fool or a madman.

He that doth any Thing in a violent Passion, is like one that puts to Sea in the midst of a Storm.

I.

Industry pays Debts, but Despair increaseth them.

If thou wouldst know a Man, lay his Words and Actions together.

If thou hast not Sense enough to speak, have Wit enough to hold thy tongue.

It is not so painful to an honest Man to want Money, as to be owing it.

It is a common Remark,—that *Love* and *Pride* stock *Bedlam*, then beware of each.

If you think twice before you speak once, you'll speak twice the better for it.

It is better to pay and have little left, than to keep much and be always in Debt.

If thou wouldst live long, live well; for two Things shorten Life, viz. *Folly* and *Wickedness.*

If thou hast a lazy Servant, send him on Errands *before* Dinner.

K.

Knowledge will not be acquired without Attention and Application.

Knowledge is a Treasure, but Judgment must be the Treasurer

Keep thy Heart close, and thy Countenance open.

Knowledge without practice in Religion, is like a Sun without light.

Know what is thy duty and do it.

Keen Razors, and sharp Speeches, have cutting effects.

Keep good Company, and thou shalt be one of the Number.

L.

Liberality is the best Way to gain Affection among the poor and needy.

Let thy Zeal for Truth be consistent with Charity

Little Wit serves to flatter with; for how easy do they Work that go with the Grain.

Lay up when thou art young, and you'll enjoy it when old.

Love thy Friend, but look to thyself.

Look not into God's Decrees, but into his Commands.

Love not the World, nor the Things of it.

Let a Man do his best, and the World do its worst.

Learning is preferable to Riches,—Virtue to both.

Let thy Vices die before thee, leave them before they leave thee.

Love may be produced by Choice, but you cannot get free from it easily.

Lies stand upon one Leg, but Truth upon two.

M.

Money is like Dung,—it does no good until it is spread, —It is the Use, and not the Possession of it, that makes us happy.

Marry not for Money only, but let Love and Money unite to make wedlock happy.

Misfortunes none are exempt from.

Money is the Miser's God which he daily worships.

Many bad Things are done only through Custom.

Merit may be hidden under a ragged coat.

More perish through too much Confidence, than too much Fear. Where one despairs, there are Thousands that presume.

Miseries are Endless, if we stand in fear of all Possibilities.

Many know not the Value of Water til the Well is dry.

N.

No Man was ever cast down by Fortune's frowns, but he suffered himself to be deceived by her Favours.

No Man is Master of himself, so long as he is a Slave to either Passion or Pleasure.

No Man is truly wise or safe, that has not the fear of God before his eyes.

Never promise what you cannot perform.

Never do any Thing you are like to repent of.

Nothing is so honourable as an old Friendship.

Necessity is the Mother of Invention.

Nobility may be without merit, as well as merit without nobility.

O.

Opinion is the chief Thing which does good or harm in the World. It is our false Opinions of Things which ruin us.

Our Pleasures, for the most Part, are short, false, and deceitful; and, like Drunkenness, revenge the Madness of one Hour, with the sad Repentance of many.

Our Happiness depends more on *mental* Content than *bodily* enjoyments.

One cannot spend Time better, than in learning to spend it well.

Only good and wise Men can be real Friends.

P.

Passions are good Servants but bad Masters.

Pride should be by young Men carefully avoided—by old

Men utterly despised—and by all Men generally discountenanced,

Pride and Ill-nature will be hated in spite of all the Wealth and Greatness in the World.

Prudence governs the Wise, but Profit the major part of Mankind.

Pretend not to govern others 'til thou canst govern thyself.

Pay well and you will never want Workmen.

Patience so strongly resembles Fortitude, that she is reputed to be either her Daughter or Sister.

Proud Men never have Friends; neither in Prosperity, because they know Nobody; or in Adversity, because then Nobody knows them.

Prosperity is not without its Troubles, nor Adversity without its Comforts.

Pride had rather go out of the Way, than walk behind.

Passion is a Sort of Fever in the Mind, which ever leaves us weaker than it found us.

Physic hath not more Remedies against the Diseases of the Body, than Reason hath Preservatives against the Passions of the Mind.

Passion makes them Fools, which otherwise are not so; and shows them to be Fools, which are so.

Parents are commonly more careful to bestow on their Children, the Art of speaking well, rather than of doing well; but their Manners ought to be their chief Concern.

The less Wisdom a Man has, the less he knows that he wants it.

R.

Riches may be admitted into our Houses, but not into our Hearts.

Rectitude of Will is a greater Ornament than brightness of Understanding; and to be divinely good, more valuable than any other Wisdom and Knowledge.

Raillery must be fine and delicate, and such as rather serves to heighten Conversation, than offend the Persons who compose the Assembly.

Rhetoric in serious Discourses is like the Flower in Corn; pleasing to those who come only for Amusement; but prejudicial to him who would reap Profit from it,

Riches are gotten with Pain, kept with Care, and lost with Grief. The Cares of Riches lie heavier upon a good Man, than the Inconveniences of an honest Poverty.

Recreations moderately used, are profitable to the Body for Health, and to the Mind for Refreshment; but is a Note of a vain Mind, to be running after every vain Pomp or Show.

Reputation is often got without Merit, and lost without Crime.

S.

Slander is like Flies, it leaps over all a Man's whole Parts, to light upon his Sores.

Spare when young, and spend when old.

Sacrifice not thy Conscience for Money

Search not a Wound too deep, lest thou make it worse,

Study more how to die than how to live.

Since you are not certain of an Hour, never throw away a Minute,

Some would be thought to do great Things, who are but Tools and Instruments; like the Fool that fancied he played upon the Organ, when he only blew the Bellows.

Some Enemies as well as Friends are necessary; they make us more Circumspect, diligent, wise, and good.

Suspicion always paints in the darkest Colours.

Suspicious Minds never want rumours to supply their Mistrust

T.

They that can overcome their Passions are greater than Alexander.

London Published by Willm Darton; Holborn Hill Octr 20. 1823.

The best Way to humble a proud Man is to take no Notice of him.

Tell a Friend his Faults, but do not blaze them. Tell not thy Secrets to thy Servant, for he will then be thy Master. —Try to be good, although the World laugh thee to scorn. —To live above our Station shews a proud Heart, and below it a narrow Soul.

Though the Coat be ever so fine that a Fool wears, it is but a Fools Coat still.

V.

Virtue is its own reward, and Vice its own punishment.

Virtue is nevertheless Venerable for being out of Fashion.

Vexation is rather taken than given; revenge never repairs an Injury, but may occasion one.

Virtue is but little encouraged, and Religion less. The best of Qualities can not pass without a *but*, to allay their Merit.

The Virtue of Prosperity, is Gratitude and Temperance; the Virtue of Adversity, is Fortitude and Resignation.

The vanity of human Life is like a River, constantly passing away, and yet constantly coming on.

Useful Knowledge can have no Enemies except the Ignorant. It cherishes Youth, delights the Aged, is an Ornament in Prosperity, and yields Comfort in Adversity.

A vindictive Temper is not only uneasy to others, but to them that have it.

Virtue scorns a Lie for its Cover, and Truth needs no Orator to recommend it.

W.

Wisdom is both desirable and attainable.

We do not want Precepts so much as Patterns; Examples are the safest and pleasantest Way of teaching.

Wisdom is oft hidden under a thread-bare Coat.

While a Man studies and practises Humility, he knows himself; but when he seeks after Dignity and Titles, he loses himself.

Worldly Glory ends with the World, and all that belongs to us, ends with our Lives. What then have we to be proud of?

Where Virtue guardeth the Citadel, Suspicion may assail, but shall never take it.

When Sin leaves us, we flatter ourselves that we leave it.

X.

Better is the Portion *in* a Wife, than *with* a Wife.

Familiar Conversation ought to be the School of Learning and good Breeding.—There is a Time when Nothing, a Time when Something, but no Time when *all* Things are o be spoken.

Y.

Young Men, when once dyed in Pleasure and Vanity will scarcely ever take any other Colour.

A talkative Fellow willing to learn of Isocrates, he asked him double his usual Price; because, said he, I must both teach you how to speak and to hold your Tongue.

If you seem to approve of another Man's Wit, he will allow you to have some Judgment.

There are a thousand Fops made by Art; for one Fool that is made by Nature.

Those who have been enriched by others Ruin, have often been ruined with their own Riches.

A Man may be a good Adviser, though an ill Solicitor.

Mercy to the Evil, proves cruelty to the Innocent.

Vice is often covered by Wealth, and Virtue by Povery.

Z.

Zeno, hearing a young Man speak too freely, told him, for this Reason we have two Ears, and but *one* Tongue, that we should hear much, and talk little.

London, Published by Will.ᵐ Darton; Holborn Hill, Oct.ʳ 20. 1823.

A Man had better be poisoned in his Blood than in his Principles.

A divided Family can no more stand, than a divided Commonwealth.

Always take Part with, and defend the Unfortunate.

Take Heed *of* whom, *what,* and *to* whom you speak.

In Marriage, prefer the Person before Wealth,—Virtue before Beauty,—and the Mind before the Body; then you will have a Wife, a Friend, and a Companion, all in *one.*

Obey the Magistrate and the Laws but not servilely. Observe Ceremonies, but not superstitiously.

Zeal without Knowledge is like Gunpowder,—soon blown in the Air.

Printed by W. Darton. jun 58, Holborn Hill.